M U H A M M A D   A L I

Published by Creative Education
123 South Broad Street
Mankato, Minnesota 56001
Creative Education is an imprint of The Creative Company.

DESIGN AND PRODUCTION **EVANSDAY DESIGN**

PHOTOGRAPHS BY Corbis (Bettmann, Robert Maass, Jeff Mitchell/Reuters, Lisa O'Connor/ZUMA,
Flip Schulke, Joseph Schwartz Collection, Tim Wright), Getty Images (Harry Benson, Brian Hamill)

The Greatest, My Own Story by Muhammad Ali with Richard Durham. Copyright © 1975
by Muhammad Ali, Herbert Muhammad, Richard Durham. Reprinted by permission.

LIBRARY OF CONGRESS CATALOGING–IN–PUBLICATION DATA
Healy, Nick.
Muhammad Ali / by Nick Healy.
p. cm. — (Genius)
Includes index.
ISBN 1-58341-333-2
1. Ali, Muhammad, 1942-–Juvenile literature. 2. Boxers (Sports)–United States–
Biography–Juvenile literature.
I. Title. II. Genius (Mankato, Minn.)

GV1132.A44H43 2004
796.83'092–dc22   2004058227 [B]

First edition

9 8 7 6 5 4 3 2 1

[M U H A M M A D   A L i]

GENiUS

Nick Healy

HE WAS THE GREATEST, AND IF BOXING FANS DIDN'T KNOW THAT,

HE WAS QUICK TO TELL THEM. AS A FRESH-FACED YOUNG FIGHTER,

MUHAMMAD ALI SEIZED THE HEAVYWEIGHT CHAMPIONSHIP BY CRUSH-

ING A MAN PREVIOUSLY CONSIDERED INDESTRUCTIBLE. WHILE CEL-

EBRATING AFTER THE MATCH, ALI SHOUTED, "I AM THE GREATEST! I

SHOOK UP THE WORLD! I'M THE GREATEST THING THAT EVER LIVED!"

HE SPENT THE REST OF HIS CAREER PROVING HE WAS RIGHT, JUST IN

CASE ANYONE DOUBTED HIM. BUT ALI WAS MORE THAN A FIGHTER.

DURING A TUMULTUOUS TIME IN AMERICAN HISTORY, HE BECAME

AN INSPIRATION TO MANY PEOPLE AND A LIGHTNING ROD FOR THE

CRITICISM OF OTHERS. HE PERSEVERED THROUGH MANY TRIALS,

TRANSFORMING FINALLY INTO A BELOVED HERO, A PEOPLE'S CHAM-

PION, AND, QUITE POSSIBLY, THE BEST HEAVYWEIGHT OF ALL TIME.

GENiUS

1   A KID FROM KENTUCKY

A segregationist sign from the 1940s

Cassius Jr. would make his name known to sports fans everywhere; then, he would leave it behind. He would become Muhammad Ali, and he would challenge every limitation placed upon him.

The time and place of Cassius's birth are important because they had a great impact on his life and his character. The Japanese attack on United States forces at Pearl Harbor, Hawaii, had occurred little more than a month earlier. Soon World War II would send Americans of all races and religions to defend freedom in Europe and across the Pacific Ocean. At home, however, people lived in what amounted to two Americas—one for white people and one for everyone else. That fact was obvious in cities such as Louisville, where African Americans were barred from many restaurants and shops and were forced to sit in the balconies of movie theaters.

Cassius's family lived a relatively comfortable life. His father worked as a sign painter, and his mother cooked and cleaned for wealthy families in other Louisville neighborhoods. Cassius had a younger brother named Rudolph, who was born in 1944. They were all part of what people then called the "black middle class," which was clearly different from the "white middle class."

In the years after World War II, middle-class whites prospered like never before. They bought new houses in the suburbs and parked new cars in their garages. Their children went to clean new schools. But the same was not true for the black middle class. People like Cassius Clay Sr., who dreamed of working as a professional artist, did not have the same opportunities as their white peers. Cassius Sr. put his talents to work where he could, painting signs for local businesses such as department stores and barbershops. The Clay family did not enjoy many luxuries, but they did not go without food, clothing, or other necessities. Many African Americans, especially those in the Deep South, could not say the same.

As he grew up, Cassius Jr. became aware of the unequal ways people were treated. At age five, he noticed that whites ran most of the shops, including ones where African Americans could shop. White people owned the drug store and the grocery store. White people drove the city buses. Finally, he asked his father, "What do the colored people do?"

At home and among friends, Cassius appeared to be a happy child. He had a quick smile and wide, bright eyes. His mother said, "By the time he was four, he had all the confidence in the world. Even when he played with older children, he always wanted to be the leader." Still, Cassius knew that outside of his neighborhood, many

Timeline **1954**   ANGER OVER A STOLEN BICYCLE LEADS THE 12-YEAR-OLD CLAY TO A BOXING GYM.

One of the first foes young Cassius Clay faced was segregation; 1940s Kentucky was still very much separated when it came to race, and blacks felt the strain.

doors would be closed to him simply because of his race. He later said, "I don't know what it was, but I always felt like I was born to do something for my people."

An injustice of sorts—a small crime—helped introduce Cassius to boxing. In October 1954, he and a friend rode their bicycles to Louisville's Columbia Auditorium, where a trade show of mostly African-American businesses was being held. They parked their bikes and went inside to enjoy free popcorn and hot dogs. When the boys returned, they discovered that Cassius's new red-and-white Schwinn had been stolen. Out-raged, Cassius ran the streets looking for his bike and whoever took it.

Someone directed Cassius to a police officer at the Columbia Gym named Joe Martin. In his free time, Martin helped train young boxers. The officer listened to Cassius's story and his promise to get revenge. Martin asked if he knew how to fight, and Cassius admitted he did not. "Why don't you learn something about fighting before you go making any hasty challenges?" Martin asked. Cassius accepted the offer and began training at the gym. Six weeks later, though only 12 years old and weighing only 89 pounds (40 kg), Cassius won his first boxing match.

CLAY WINS HIS FIRST NATIONAL GOLDEN GLOVES AND AMATEUR ATHLETIC ASSOCIATION CHAMPIONSHIPS. *Timeline* **1959**

The theft of 12-year-old Clay's bike drove the youngster to the gym, where he took up the sport that would make him wealthy and famous.

RISING IN THE RANKS

CASSIUS CLAY MADE A REMARKABLE RISE IN BOXING, BUT HIS FIRST MATCH WAS FAR FROM PRETTY. HE AND A BOY NAMED RONNIE O'KEEFE, BOTH EQUIPPED WITH OVERSIZED GLOVES, TRADED PUNCHES FOR THREE ROUNDS. IN THE END, CASSIUS WAS DECLARED THE WINNER BECAUSE HE LANDED A FEW MORE BLOWS. SOON, HOWEVER, CASSIUS DEMONSTRATED HIS EXCEPTIONAL TALENT.

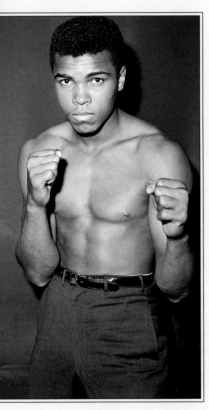

The 20-year-old "Louisville Slugger"

He fought many amateur bouts as a teenager, and he developed a style that later made him famous. He danced around the ring on his toes, always circling and keeping his opponent on the move. He held his hands low, appearing to leave himself unguarded. And he had an uncanny ability to dodge trouble, leaning his head back at the last possible moment and watching punches swoosh past.

Boxing became the center of Cassius's life. He swore off junk food and devoted himself to training. Sometimes, he would put in six hours a day—jogging each morning, working out at Martin's gym, and fine-tuning his skills. Cassius's appearances on a Louisville television show called "Tomorrow's Champions" made him a local celebrity. Each week, the show featured matches between the city's top amateur boxers, and Cassius routinely beat the best, including boys who were older, bigger, and more experienced.

During Cassius's teen years, athletics overshadowed academics. He struggled at Central High, where poor grades forced him to repeat the 10th grade. When he finally graduated in June 1960, Cassius was near the bottom of his class, likely because he devoted so much free time to training and so little to studying. The gym also provided an escape from a home life that was not always easy. Cassius's father was known to drink too much, and the alcohol sometimes made him violent. Cassius Sr. had a long record with Louisville police, including three charges of domestic abuse filed by his wife.

By age 18, Cassius Jr. was an experienced fighter. His amateur record was 100 wins and 8 losses. He was a two-time national Gold Gloves champion for his weight class, and a two-time national Amateur Athletic Union champion. He also exhibited the loud, brash personality he would be known for later in life. He talked and talked and talked. Sometimes he made short rhymes predicting doom for opponents or poking fun at them. "This guy must be done. I'll stop him in one," he said. Nobody was surprised if he knocked out his opponent in the first round as predicted.

The 1960 Olympics in Rome, Italy, provided an international stage for Cassius. He had grown into a lean, muscular young man, and he was considered among America's best hopes for a medal in boxing. Fighting in the light-heavyweight division, designated for those weighing 178 pounds (80 kg), Cassius breezed through his first three matches, earning a chance at the gold medal. In the finals, he defeated Polish fighter Zbigniew Pietrzykowski in a tough match that left the Pole bloodied and barely able to stay on his feet.

"Ali spent all his time in the gym. That's where he lived. He wanted to box, and he wanted to be great. And that's what his life was all about."

JIMMY ELLIS
FELLOW LOUISVILLE FIGHTER AND
EVENTUAL HEAVYWEIGHT CHAMPION

Upon returning home from the 1960 Olympics in Rome with a gold medal, Clay was greeted by his mother Odessa and brother Rudy.

Cassius received a hero's welcome when he went back to Louisville. A rally celebrating his return was held at Central High, the site of many earlier struggles. At home, where the front steps were freshly painted red, white, and blue, Cassius's mother prepared a turkey dinner while his father showed off his son to neighbors and sang "God Bless America" on the porch. Still, Cassius found he was not welcome everywhere in his hometown. Soon after, the Olympic gold medalist sat down at a lunch counter and asked for a glass of juice. The owner refused to serve Cassius because he was an African American.

Higher aspirations filled Cassius's mind soon after his Olympic victory; he wanted nothing less than the heavyweight championship. His first professional bout came in October 1960, when he beat a little-known fighter named Tunney Hunsaker. And it didn't take long—two and a half years and 19 fights—for Cassius to prove himself ready to take on the best, a fearsome fighter named Sonny Liston. The heavyweight champion was a big man and a powerful hitter, but Cassius poked fun at him, calling him a "big ugly bear," and predicted the champ would not last beyond the eighth round. When the two fighters squared off in February 1964, most fans expected Liston to teach the young loudmouth a lesson. They were in for a surprise.

MALCOLM X AND HIS FAMILY STAY AT CLAY'S HOME AFTER MALCOLM X RECEIVES DEATH THREATS. *Timeline* **1964**

*Following his Olympic success, Clay hired master motivator Angelo Dundee (left)
to become his trainer; the two formed a boxing partnership that lasted 21 years.*

3 FIGHTING WITH PURPOSE

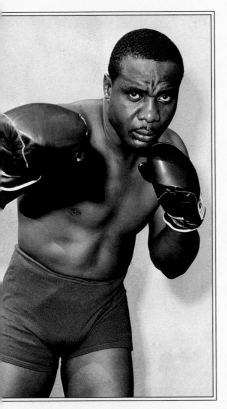

Two-time heavyweight champ Sonny Liston

Revealing his strategy in the ring, Cassius and one of his corner men chanted, "Float like a butterfly, sting like a bee!" When Liston stepped off the scale (he outweighed the taller Cassius), Cassius shouted, "I'm gonna whup you so bad! You're a chump!" Liston hardly knew how to respond.

The same could be said of what happened in the ring that night. In the first round, Liston unleashed a barrage of wild swings. Cassius dodged and danced, then found openings and fired back, landing hard blows that got the attention of everyone in the Miami Beach Convention Hall. In the second round, Cassius's jab opened a cut under Liston's left eye. When the bell sounded to begin the seventh round, Liston remained in his corner. He could fight no more. Celebration erupted among Cassius and his supporters, while reporters and many in the crowd sat stunned. "I am the king!" Cassius shouted. "King of the world!"

For boxing fans, another surprise was yet to come. While talking with reporters after the fight, Cassius acknowledged that he

DESPITE 7-1 ODDS AGAINST HIM, CLAY DEFEATS SONNY LISTON TO BECOME HEAVYWEIGHT CHAMPION.   *Timeline* 1964

had become a member of the Nation of Islam, a group led by a man named Elijah Muhammad. Soon after, the group's leader welcomed Cassius, and in a speech broadcast on the radio, explained that the name "Cassius Clay" had no "divine meaning," and the fighter would take a new name, "Muhammad Ali."

"Imagine it for a moment. The heavyweight champion, a magical man, taking his fight out of the ring and into the arena of politics, and standing firm. The message that sent!"

SONIA SANCHEZ
POET AND CIVIL RIGHTS ADVOCATE

The new champion's devotion to the Nation of Islam was no small matter in the America of the 1960s. At that time, African Americans were fighting for rights long denied them. A century after slavery had ended, they still suffered widespread discrimination. In some places, they were denied the right to vote and were barred from restaurants and hotels. Martin Luther King Jr. led protests seeking equality through integration, with all races living together. The Nation of Islam, however, believed African Americans were better off living separately, strengthening their own communities.

The Nation of Islam was disliked by many whites and a good number of African Americans who believed the group's message increased tension between the races. Sportswriters around the country criticized Muhammad's religious conversion. Even Muhammad's parents were displeased at the news. Cassius Sr. said the Nation of Islam had "conned" his son.

Still, the name "Muhammad Ali" soon became famous around the world. Shortly after winning the title, Muhammad toured the Middle East and Africa, greeting cheering fans and meeting the leaders of several nations. In the African country of Ghana, Muhammad said, "I'm glad to be here with my true people." Crowds of children chanted, "Ali! Ali! Ali!"

Timeline **1964**   CLAY CHANGES HIS NAME TO "MUHAMMAD ALI" TO REFLECT HIS CONVERSION TO THE ISLAMIC FAITH.

Dr. Martin Luther King Jr. blazed a path for African Americans during the civil rights movement of the 1960s; Ali also became involved in the struggle.

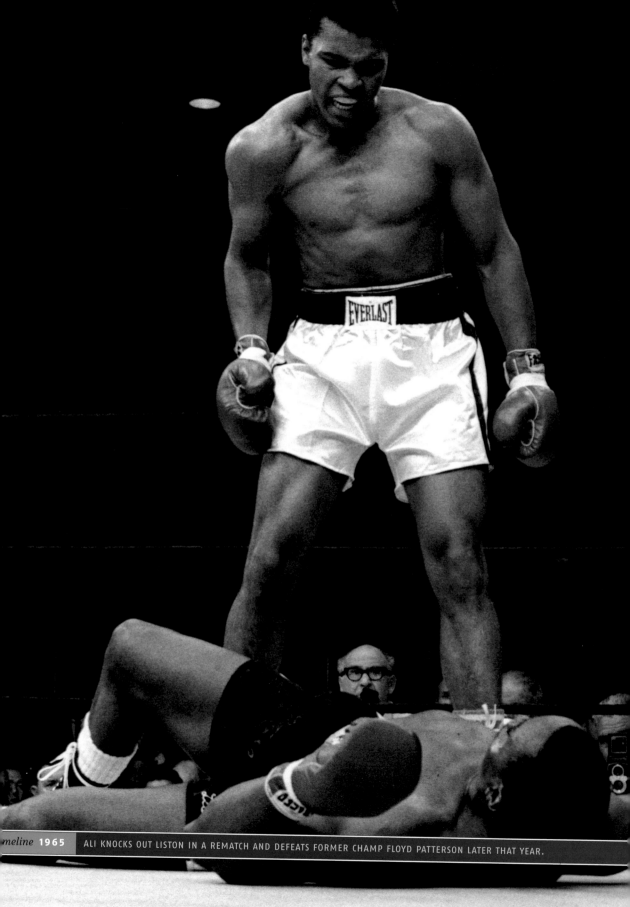

Matters in America still demanded the champ's attention, however. In the summer of 1964, Muhammad fell in love with a woman named Sonji Roi. She later said that Muhammad asked her to marry him the first night they met. As it turned out, the wedding came just 41 days later, on August 14, 1964. But Muhammad also had a title to defend. A rematch with Liston came first. The two met again in May 1965, and Muhammad scored a first-round knockout with a quick right hand to Liston's temple. Soon after that fight, Muhammad's brief marriage ended. He asked the court for an annulment—voiding the marriage as though it had never happened—because he claimed that Sonji did not fulfill a promise to follow the laws of the Nation of Islam.

After defending his title nine times, Muhammad finally lost his championship belt, but not at the hands of another fighter. With U.S. troops at war in Vietnam, Muhammad had been drafted. However, he said his religion barred him from going to war, and he refused induction into the armed forces. Boxing's governing organizations responded by stripping him of his title in May 1967. Muhammad stood firm, even when charged with a felony for avoiding service and even in the face of stinging criticism from reporters, politicians, and many in the public. "Many great men have been tested for their religious beliefs," Muhammad said. "If I pass this test, I'll come out stronger than ever."

ALI ENDS HIS BRIEF MARRIAGE TO SONJI ROI, CONTENDING THE MARRIAGE WENT AGAINST HIS RELIGION. | *Timeline* **1965**

In one of American sports' most famous photos, Ali hovers triumphantly over a fallen Sonny Liston during their 1965 title fight in Lewiston, Maine.

RUMBLE IN THE JUNGLE

MUHAMMAD WAS JUST 25 YEARS OLD WHEN STRIPPED OF HIS TITLE, AND HIS LONG JOURNEY BACK TO THE TOP BECAME HIS TOUGHEST TEST. AFTER HE REFUSED THE MILITARY DRAFT, HIS CRITICS STIRRED PUBLIC OUTRAGE AGAINST HIM; BOXING COMMISSIONS IN EVERY STATE TOOK AWAY HIS LICENSE TO FIGHT. FOR MORE THAN THREE YEARS, MUHAMMAD ENDURED WHAT HE CALLED HIS "EXILE" FROM THE SPORT.

Joe Frazier whiffing at Ali, 1971

Muhammad kept busy during his time away. In August 1967, he married for a second time. His new wife was 17-year-old Belinda Boyd, who had grown up as a devoted follower of Islam. Muhammad also traveled across the country to give lectures on college campuses about boxing, the war, and the beliefs of the Nation of Islam. When finally allowed back into the ring in 1970, many fans wondered if Muhammad's best boxing days were behind him.

In March 1971, Muhammad squared off against undefeated heavyweight champion Joe Frazier in New York City's Madison Square Garden. Millions of people around the world watched on television as the two traded withering punches through the 15-round match. In the final round, a left hook from Frazier downed Muhammad, who rose to his feet and hung on until the final bell. The judges unanimously declared Frazier the winner.

Earning another title fight would not be easy. Muhammad fought and won 10 straight matches before losing to Ken Norton in March 1973. The loss forced a grueling rematch later that year, which Muhammad won by judges' decision. In the meantime, Frazier had lost his title to George Foreman, suffering a knockout. Muhammad and Frazier fought a second time early in 1974, and after 12 tough rounds, Muhammad was declared the winner. That set up a match with Foreman.

The meeting of Muhammad and Foreman was no ordinary championship bout. It was scheduled to take place in an outdoor stadium in Kinshasa, Zaire (a central African nation now called The Democratic Republic of Congo). The location, which inspired promoters to label the match "The Rumble in the Jungle," suited Muhammad, who celebrated his African heritage and won fans during his travels across the continent. "It's a great feeling being in a country operated by black people," the 32-year-old said. "I wish all black people in America could see this."

Foreman presented a serious challenge for Muhammad. The champion was undefeated, with 37 knockouts in 40 professional fights. He was seven years younger than Muhammad, and sportswriters speculated that Foreman hit harder than any heavyweight in history. While the fighters spent weeks in Zaire training before the match, Muhammad seemed confident as usual. "Float like a butterfly, sting like a bee," he said. "His hands can't hit what his eyes can't see."

> "The speeches were important, not just for Ali but for everyone who heard them. He was leading people into areas of thought and information that might not otherwise have been accessible to them."
>
> ROBERT LIPSYTE
> SPORTSWRITER

Timeline **1971**   THE SUPREME COURT THROWS OUT ALI'S DRAFT-DODGING CONVICTION; ALI LOSES TO JOE FRAZIER.

Fighting with a broken jaw, Ali tried to protect his face from Ken Norton in a March 1973 fight that Norton went on to win; Ali won a rematch later that year.

> *"I hit him with punches that'd bring down the walls of a city. It was like death. Closest thing to dying that I know of."*
>
> JOE FRAZIER
> AFTER HIS 1971 WIN
> OVER MUHAMMAD

> *"I won't kid you. When he went into the ropes, I felt sick. Going into the fight, I thought Muhammad would win but not that way."*
>
> ANGELO DUNDEE
> MUHAMMAD'S TRAINER, ON
> THE 1974 FOREMAN BOUT

Due to the difference in time zones, the fight started at 3:00 A.M. in Zaire to suit closed-circuit television audiences in America. Chanting "*Ali, bomaye!*" ("Ali, kill him!"), most fans in the stadium stood firmly behind the challenger. At the opening bell, Muhammad went straight at Foreman and got his attention with a solid blow to the head; then, Muhammad danced away and tried to use his quickness against Foreman. Even Muhammad's supporters figured the only way he could win was to stay on the run until Foreman grew tired. But Muhammad decided that was not going to work. "After the first round, I used more energy staying away from him than he used chasing me," he said.

Muhammad then did something that nobody expected. In the following rounds, he let Foreman back him into the ropes, and he stayed there. Muhammad called the strategy "rope-a-dope," meaning he would let his opponent foolishly waste energy by throwing punches that did little damage. Muhammad leaned back into the ropes, keeping his chin out of Foreman's reach, and used his forearms and elbows to block many of Foreman's body blows. "I was on the ropes, but he was trapped because attacking was all he knew how to do," Muhammad said.

At the start of round eight, Muhammad thought, "Now it's my turn." Late in the round, he landed a series of powerful rights, and Foreman's body buckled. Foreman staggered around the ring and finally fell to the canvas. Muhammad raised his hands as the champion once again.

ALI IS NAMED *SPORTS ILLUSTRATED*'S SPORTSMAN OF THE YEAR; SOME CALL 1974 THE PINNACLE OF ALI'S CAREER. *Timeline* 1974

In the "Rumble in the Jungle," Ali implemented his famous "rope-a-dope" strategy; round eight saw Ali come alive to attack and floor the powerful George Foreman.

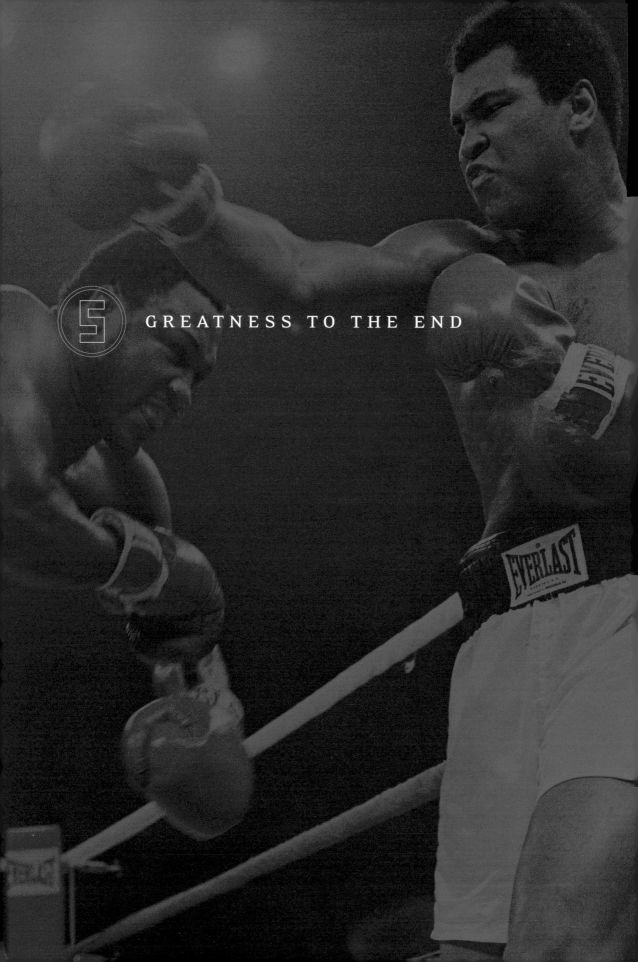

GREATNESS TO THE END

MUHAMMAD HAD CONSIDERED MAKING THE FIGHT HIS LAST AND RETIRING, WIN OR LOSE. IT HAD BEEN 10 YEARS SINCE HE BEAT SONNY LISTON TO CLAIM THE TITLE AND 7 YEARS SINCE IT HAD BEEN TAKEN FROM HIM. FOR A BOXER, MUHAMMAD WAS FAR FROM A YOUNG MAN, YET HE REVELED IN HIS RETURN TO HIS SPORT'S PINNACLE.

Ali (left) and Foreman in 1997

"Now that I've got my championship back, every day is something special," he said. The public seemed to share Muhammad's enthusiasm. Newspapers and magazines that once criticized him for his political and religious beliefs now embraced him. *Ring* magazine declared him "Fighter of the Year," and *Sports Illustrated* made him its "Sportsman of the Year."

Each subsequent fight brought in a big paycheck—$1 million or more—for the champion. Eventually, a third match was scheduled between Muhammad and Joe Frazier. The first had gone to Frazier; the second to Muhammad. Their rivalry had grown intense by the time they stepped into the ring in October 1975, with Muhammad taunting Frazier and calling him a "gorilla." The fight took place in the Philippines, resulting in its billing as the "Thrilla in Manila."

Muhammad's personal life was in turmoil at the time. He traveled to the Philippines with a woman named Veronica Porche at his side, leaving his wife, Belinda, and their children back in the

States. When newspaper reporters wrote about Muhammad's new companion, Belinda flew to Manila to confront her husband. It was the beginning of the end of Muhammad's second marriage. He would later marry Veronica, but at the time, he had to put his troubles aside and focus on Frazier.

The fight lived up to its name—going 14 mesmerizing rounds before Frazier admitted defeat—and is remembered as one of the greatest boxing matches of all time. It was also the last great fight of Muhammad's career. He lost his title to a young, talented boxer named Leon Spinks in 1978 but won it back in a rematch, making Muhammad the first three-time heavyweight champion. He retired soon thereafter, although he later came back for two forgettable losses before quitting for good in 1981. His final record was 56 wins (with 37 knockouts) and 5 losses.

Muhammad's life during the first few years after boxing was difficult. His marriage to Veronica was in trouble, and the couple eventually divorced in 1986. But Muhammad started experiencing physical difficulties, too. Although the cause of his problems was at first unknown, he clearly was not the person he had once been. His speech became slow and slurred, and his movement seemed sluggish, no longer full of grace and power. Muhammad was eventually diagnosed with Parkinson's syndrome, a neurological problem that causes tremors and slow speech. The disorder was likely caused by trauma to the brain resulting from the thousands of punches he absorbed while boxing.

> *"Muhammad amazed me; I'll admit it. He out-thought me; he out-fought me. That night, he was just the better man in the ring. Before the fight, I thought I'd knock him out easy."*
>
> GEORGE FOREMAN
> ON HIS 1974 MATCH WITH MUHAMMAD

Timeline **1979** ALI, HAVING REGAINED HIS TITLE FROM LEON SPINKS IN A REMATCH, RETIRES FROM THE RING.

Ali poses in front of a collection of Time *magazine covers; since his retirement from boxing, he has become one of America's best-loved sports figures.*

MARCH 9, 1998 $3.95
TIME
TIME
The Poisoning of America
When the Music Died
John Lennon
PLANET OF THE YEAR
Whew!
America Returns to Space
everything you always wanted to know about
woody allen
THE GUN IN AMERICA
MAN ON THE MOON
WHY
THELMA & LOUISE
STRIKES A NERVE

Still, happiness returned to Muhammad's life. He married again, this time to a woman he had known since she was a child. Lonnie Williams's family lived across the street from Muhammad's parents in Louisville. It was Muhammad's fourth marriage, and he acknowledged mistakes in younger years and in earlier marriages, including his shortcomings as a father to a total of nine children. "Because of the divorces and the way I lived, I wasn't really around to raise them. But they turned out good," he said. "And whatever they need, I try to give it to them."

Parkinson's syndrome has had a significant impact on Muhammad's mobility, but his personality and spirit remain much the same. Once loud and bold, he now speaks little and moves with great care, but he continues to travel the world to greet his fans. In one memorable moment, Muhammad carried the Olympic torch up a long flight of stadium steps, despite trembling in his arms and legs, and lit the Olympic Flame to begin the 1996 Summer Games in Atlanta, Georgia. Millions of people around the world watched the celebration of Muhammad and his accomplishments.

Muhammad was back in the public eye in 2004, when he walked onto the field to deliver the ball for the ceremonial first pitch at Major League Baseball's All-Star Game. The crowd cheered as Muhammad, his eyes wide, clowned and threw soft punches into the air. The man who had been so controversial in his youth was now perhaps the most beloved sports figure of his time.

CROWDS CHEER ALI AS HE CARRIES THE OLYMPIC TORCH AT THE OPENING OF THE SUMMER GAMES IN ATLANTA, GEORGIA. Timeline 1996

Ali occasionally pops up in public since his boxing career ended, as he did in an appearance at the 2004 Major League Baseball All-Star Game in Houston.

IN HIS

W O R D S

IN THE MID-1970S, A BOOK DESCRIBED AS MUHAMMAD ALI'S

AUTOBIOGRAPHY WAS RELEASED, ALTHOUGH IT WAS WRITTEN

LARGELY BY RICHARD DURHAM, EDITOR OF THE NATION OF

ISLAM'S NEWSPAPER. PORTIONS OF DURHAM'S TEXT ARE NOW

CONSIDERED MYTH OR LEGEND, ENHANCED BY THE WRITER TO

BUILD THE IMAGE OF HIS SUBJECT. BUT MUCH OF THE BOOK IS

ACCURATE, OF COURSE, AND MANY DETAILED ACCOUNTS OF EVENTS

INSIDE THE RING COULD HAVE COME ONLY FROM ALI. IN THE

FOLLOWING EXCERPTS FROM *THE GREATEST*, ALI DESCRIBES THE

SCENE BEFORE THE BELL SOUNDED TO BEGIN "THE RUMBLE IN THE

JUNGLE" AND HIS THOUGHTS IN THE MOMENTS AFTER THE FIGHT.

The champion is coming down the aisle, his entourage around him. His hands are up in the Olympic salute. I watch him climb up the steps behind his crew, Dick Sadler, Archie Moore, Sandy Saddler. He goes immediately to his stool. He doesn't move about the ring to get the feel of it. He doesn't test the ropes or get the feel of the crowd. He slumps on his stool and will stay there until the referee comes to the center of the ring.

I dance lightly and steadily. I glance across the ring and see Sadler whispering in George's ear. Now Zack Clayton, the referee, comes to the center. George is poised to get up.

The referee motions to us.

The greatest roar I've ever heard fills the air. We stand up face to face.

"ALI! ALI! BOMAYE!

[ALI! ALI! KILL HIM!]

ALI! ALI! BOMAYE!"

"FOREMAN! FOREMAN!

THE CHAMPION! THE CHAMPION!"

"ALI! ALI! BOMAYE!

ALI! ALI! BOMAYE!"

Our eyes are locked like gunfighters' in a Wild West movie. . . . In his eyes, I see Sonny Liston glaring at me 10 years ago at Miami Beach, a fresh, young, powerful, taller, stronger Liston. Now I think this will answer the question critics have been asking since I first won the title from an "aging Liston":

Could I have defeated a young Sonny Liston?

Clayton [the referee] begins his instructions. "Now both of you know the rules. When I step back, you break clean. No hitting on the breaks...."

But I draw my guns first. I lean close to George's ear, and since I obviously have his undivided attention, I think we should get a few things straight that the referee might overlook. "Chump," I say with all the contempt I can muster. "You're gonna get yourself beat tonight in front of all these Africans."

The referee's head jerks up. "Ali, no talking! Listen to the instructions." He goes on. "No hitting below the belt. No kidney punches...."

"Never mind that stuff, sucker." I speak low. "I'm gonna hit you everywhere but under the bottom of your big funky feet, chump! You got to go, sucker!"

"Ali, I warned you," the referee snaps. "Be quiet!"

George bites his lips, and his eyes glare.

"Ref," I say. "This sucker is in trouble. He ain't nobody's champ!"

George's eyes go from me to the referee. He wants Clayton to chastise me, but I pull his eyes back to mine. The referee talks on mechanically while I say to George, "You heard about me for years, sucker! All your life you been hearing about Muhammad Ali. Now, chump, you gotta face me!"

"Ali, I'm warning you for the last time!"

George's eyes are tight. His head is close to mine.

"You been hearing about how bad I am since you were a little kid with mess in your pants! Tonight"—I say it loud—"I'm gonna whip you until you cry like a baby."

"If you don't stop talking, I'll disqualify you." Clayton is furious; his hands shake. "I want a good, clean, sportsman fight, or I will absolutely call a halt to it."

"That's the only way you gonna save this sucker," I say. "He's doomed!"

Sweat is coming down George's forehead. Archie Moore is rubbing his shoulders.

"If you talk while fighting," the referee says, "I'm going to stop this fight, you hear? I'll stop it!"

I've been told this before, but where does it say in the rules that fighters can't have an orderly discussion while they work as long as they perform properly? Where does it say that they cannot discuss some personal problems or world problems?

The only other time objections were raised to my talking was when I fought Oscar Bonavena in Madison Square Garden, and the New York Boxing Commissioner, [Edwin] Dooley, put in a special rule aimed at me which declared that if either fighter talked during the fight a fine of $5,000 would be levied, which I thought was a compliment, since Bonavena understands no English and I speak no Spanish.

I keep talking. Too much is at stake to stop this fight. Too much has gone into making it; a billion people around the world are watching it. I'm not worried about the referee. After all, he knows I will not neglect my work while I lecture George. I will enlighten his mind while I whip him. The public will not be cheated. In fact, I will perform even better than if I go out slugging like a deadpan Frankenstein robot.

"Sucker," I explain, "I'm too fast for a big, slow mummy. Your title is gone. You never should have come to Africa."

"All right, all right!" Clayton gives up. "Go to your corners and come out fighting when you hear the bell, and may the best man …"

I flip around and dance to my corner. The thunderous roars come in waves, chants, yells, shouts.

"ALI! ALI! BOMAYE!"

"FOREMAN! THE CHAMPION!"

I've never fought in a stadium like this. I feel at home. So much so, I look across at George and take his measurements as though I'm his undertaker's tailor, outfitting him for the suit he's to wear in his casket. How soon shall I go all out? How soon shall I gamble on getting him in the half-dream?

I've called it the half-dream room since I was a boy, boxing in Louisville, and was knocked down and almost out in the gym for the first time. I went home and thought about it all night. I had seen champions, contenders, professional boxers on TV get knocked down and out. Now I knew how it felt.

It's like in the Golden Gloves tournaments. I'm hit, knocked groggy. The feeling is like being half awake and half dreaming. And your awake half knows what you're dreaming about. In fact, it follows the whole scene. A heavy blow takes you to the door of this room. It opens, and you see neon, orange and green lights blinking. You see bats blowing trumpets, alligators play trombones, and snakes are screaming. Weird masks and actor's clothes hang on the wall.

The first time the blow sends you there, you panic and run, but when you wake up you say, "Well, since it was only a dream, why didn't I play it cool, put on the actor's clothes, the mask, and see what it's like?" Only you have to fix it in your mind and plan to do it long before the half-dream comes. For when it comes, time stretches out slow. You have to put the plan in your mind long before you need it. The blow makes your mind vibrate like a tuning fork. You can't let your opponent follow up. You've got to stop the fork from vibrating.

I know how to do it now, like when Frazier knocked me down in the 15th round. I get up groggy. I go on the defensive. I act until my head clears, as I did when [Ken] Norton broke my jaw in the second round and opened the door of the half-dream room. I acted it out until the fight was over.

I know George has never been hurt or dazed. He has never been behind in a single round. Shall I gamble in the first round? When should I go all out to take him to the dream room? Will he know what to do? Has the champion thought it out as I have?

George is on his feet, but it's over. The referee raises my hand in victory.

And the stadium explodes. People break past the paratroopers and climb over the press tables, climb into the ring.

Archie [Moore] has wrapped his arms around George, and I holler, "Archie, am I too old?"

Archie jerks his head my way. There's a gleam in his eye. He raises his fists and shouts, "Your time is coming! Your day will come!"

And this I know. But the referee is raising my hand, and the whole world is screaming, "Ali! Ali! Ali! Ali!"

A reporter claws his way through the crowd and yells at me, "How did you do it, World Heavyweight Champion? What do you think of George now?"

I shake my head. I want to go to my dressing room. I don't want to tell him what George has taught me. That too many victories weaken you. That the defeated can rise up stronger than the victor.

But I take nothing away from George. He can still beat any man in the world.

Except me.

CIVIL RIGHTS   Legal freedoms and protections provided to citizens by their government. In the 1960s, African Americans fought for and won rights equal to their white neighbors.

EXILE   Generally means that someone has been ejected from his or her home country. Muhammad Ali used the word to describe his forced removal from boxing in the late 1960s.

FLOYD PATTERSON   The first two-time heavyweight champion. He lost the title for good in 1962, when Sonny Liston knocked him out. He later lost two bouts against Muhammad Ali. He held a career record of 55 wins, 8 losses, and 1 draw.

GOLDEN GLOVES   Amateur boxing championships that take place each year. States have their own Golden Gloves tournaments, and the winners go on to compete in the national Golden Gloves Tournament of Champions.

JOE FRAZIER   Heavyweight champion from 1970 to 1973. He dealt Ali his first professional loss in 1971, but Ali won two later fights. He held a career record of 32 wins, 4 losses, and 1 draw.

KEN NORTON   Heavyweight who fought Muhammad Ali three times in the 1970s. He defeated Ali in 1973 but lost two later fights. He briefly held the World Boxing Council heavyweight title in 1978. He held a career record of 42 wins, 7 losses, and 1 draw.

NATION OF ISLAM A religious organization founded during the 1930s in the United States. The group favors political, social, and economic independence for African Americans.

ROUND The three-minute period during which boxers compete. The number of rounds in a match varies, depending on whether the fight is amateur or professional and whether a championship is at stake.

SONNY LISTON Heavyweight champion from 1962 to 1964. He lost his title to Muhammad Ali and lost again in a rematch. He held a career record of 50 wins and 4 losses.

TRAINER A boxer's coach and instructor, the leader of his corner crew.